salmonpoetry

Memory of Blue

Jacqueline Kolosov

Published in 2014 by
Salmon Poetry
Cliffs of Moher, County Clare, Ireland
Website: www.salmonpoetry.com
Email: info@salmonpoetry.com

ISBN 978-1-908836-75-5

COVER IMAGE: "Footsteps, Mont Saint Michel, France, 1982." © William Clift 1982. Reproduced with permission of the artist.
COVER DESIGN & TYPESETTING: *Siobhán Hutson*
Printed in Ireland by Sprint Print

For Sophia and Her Father

And in Memory of
Margaret Sheffield Lutherer,
1950-2012

We are the birds that stay
—EMILY DICKINSON

Acknowledgements

Abiding thanks to the editors of the journals and anthologies in which these poems first appeared:

"Memory of Blue" and "Incarnate" in *Water~stone Review*; "Revelatory" in *Tiferet*; "Morning Song," "Ordinary," "Daughter, Here," and "Valentine" in *Poetry East*; "Quickening" in *Orion*; "Aubade," "Heights," and "Jonquils" in *Adanna*; "Kitchen Haiku" and "Skein" in *Ruah*; "Maryam" and "Plain Air" in *Literature & Belief*; "Mi Se" in *Cave Wall*; "Rain's Offering" and "Teaspoon" in *Quiddity: An International Journal*; "Little Tesuque" in *Fourth River*; "Surrender" and "Candela" in *Borderlands*; "Art Lesson: Julie Manet Walks With Renoir" and "Rereading the Velveteen Rabbit" in *Alabama Literary Journal*; "December Prayer" and "Preparation" in *The Southern Review*; "Poised" in *Sou'wester*; "Harvest" in *Into the Teeth of the Wind*; "Abide with Me" in *Confrontation*; "Locomotion" in *SLANT*; "Shelter" in *Dogs Singing: A Tribute Anthology* (Salmon Poetry, Ireland, 2010).

A selection of these poems was published as *Quickening*, a chapbook, which won White Eagle Coffee House Press's 2007 Award. A second selection, *Hourglass*, also a chapbook, was published by Pecan Grove Press in February 2012. I want to express my gratitude here to H. Palmer Hall, the Editor of Pecan Grove Press, who believed so deeply in poetry, and died in February 2013.

Thanks and gratitude to William Clift for allowing his work to grace the cover of *Memory of Blue*. My ongoing gratitude to Texas Tech University for time, support and funds; to my colleagues and students, all of whom continue to teach and to inspire me. My 3 dogs and I wag our tails with joy and thanks that the indomitable Jessie Lendennie and Siobhán Hutson have brought this book into being.

So many friends and family sustain my poetry. A special thank you to Wendy Barker, Loren Graham, Frannie Lindsay, JuanJuan Chen Henderson, Darcy Reich, Kirsten Sundberg Lunstrum; and to my husband, William Wenthe, who commented on so many of these poems—all my love. To Patty Sadler, Ashleigh Willems and Paula Sexton, for sharing with me the wisdom that is horses, and to my Marah. To my parents: thank you for your love; to my daughter, Sophia, you renew and challenge and humble me every day. All of you continue to teach me to see. Blessings.

Contents

III.

IV.

The Memory of Blue

Window opening onto adoration,
onto the lost songs of nomads once come
to illuminate glass: the raw materials
of a veiled faith brought forth
from forested places where strange spirits dwelt.

How can it be (only the ghosts of their campfires
remaining, the ash that transformed sand
into fractured heaven)—how can it be their voices
still give height to sky's luster,
still swathe a virgin girl in mystery
kin to the flutes of this morning's glories
enshrining the rusty chain link fence
and garden woodpile?

    Even this late in the day
the ultramarine light of blue remains
immaculate, despite the smoke of war
and the countless sorrows of these militant years
far away from Sar-e-Sang, fabled valley
veined with lapis lazuli's stars,
a firmament before which Titian wept
as he painted a pure cascade disappearing

in a frame. Michelangelo, too,
yearned for this blue, patiently waiting out
the echoing chimes and praying for its arrival.
How long he waited,
drinking sharp wine from a gold-lipped cup.

The Florentine sun hung low in the sky,
and the place where light kissed the horizon
opened onto the one color holy as sacrament,
the one color become looking glass,
or window, onto all that remains
the unfinished vision.

I

What need—
yet to sing love,
love must first shatter us.

H. D.

Incarnate

Just a girl really, one who must have loved
the touch of sun on her shoulders
as she sat beside the Iyon, her feet trailing the water,
a few brave fish spiriting around her toes.

Where was she when the angel appeared to her,
the whiteness of his wings more terrible
than the Word with which he anointed her?

A girl most ordinary, beloved by an ordinary man,
her parentage unmarked, until the spirit overshadowed her.

May it be to me as you have said,
she is said to have told the angel.
Afterwards, she found her way to Nazareth,
a white village on a hillside,
enclosed by mountains, as the rose is by leaves.

How much could she have known
as she followed that road through Galilee,
the same road her son, years later, would also walk?
When she stood on that road and kissed him, now grown
to a man, goodbye,
how much did she remember?
How much could she foresee?

Supremely obedient, they call Mary,
who first nursed her child among donkeys and cows.
By then, the memory of the Nazarene cliffs
must have become as familiar as the angel's face,
that annihilating brightness.
And always, after that,
she must have heard, in the wind, the beating
of his wings. *You have found favor with God.*

The road through Galilee opens onto the Roman Road.
The rose, enclosed by leaves, bears thorns.

How could she, just a girl really, have said no?

Revelatory

Before the fly-
   catcher flicked up
       into the astonished
light, we drifted,
   weightless

as the starred wood-
   candle, patient
       as the mariposa's
mottled heart. Or
   before there was

a heart to count
   the beats between
       seed and trembling
aspen, when we
   were quiet together.

Quiet as an alpine
   meadow when
       even the wind
begins to listen
   to the silence

within the crimson
   pulse of shadow,
       the tumbled
arc of hatchling's
   wing. When even

the wind begins
　　to listen
　　　　to the white
sheen of trillium's
　　precision of eye,

who we are
　　or who we might be
　　　　whistles in
and out of
　　the coniferous dark.

Morning Song

Eighteenth Week of Pregnancy

This morning I dream an aubade
within a lullaby. July's air
is leaf-wrapped, the trees all soft-
spined, the kingfisher's child
giddily unmoored.

You, whose hand-span is smaller
than a caraway seed, could nest inside
a muskmelon.

How I hope to coax the day larger, longer—

You, whose landscape is a lake-
shape, have yet to meet the kingfisher,
have yet to see him dive and rise
from milk-blue water—endless water
that teaches diaphanous perspective.

From this journey, we three will return
changed, the rooms all turned
to stained glass, the sunfish's body
sewn through with waves.

Soul

If the soul arrives
on the hundred and twentieth day
after conception, I'm on the verge
of welcoming you, soul
of my coming child.

In German, soul is *Innere*,
interior word close as
the image of you, created
not by sight but by sound's
ultrasonic waves—impossible
to explain what I felt
watching you turn to reveal
an ear too impossibly small
to conceive. All of you,
four ounces, four inches,
ten fingers, ten toes,
curled inside of me.

Innere found above *innerst*—
innermost soul
of my coming child.

To you, I want to explain
why butterflies see purple,
not red; how saffron can be
both red and yellow.

But all that comes is the image
of two sisters whispering
beneath the dining room table.
"Do black cats have tails?"
"No," replies the younger,
assured because the older sister asked.

Quickening

Twenty Weeks and Two Days

Amid the camaraderie of starlings, morning
ripens along with tomatoes on the vine.
A single twist at the stem, and summer
falls into my hands, another garden's
perfume of lemon balm and sage
between my fingertips, my mother's
kerchiefed face. August ripens,
tomatoes lavishing beside gooseberries'
fairytale orbs. Always, the robins
and the sparrows picnicked on the fattest
of the translucent fruit my mother,
with sandy cupfuls of sugar,
simmered into jam I spread on toast,
barefoot and caramel-kneed
beneath the patio's canopy of sun.
But tomatoes we always ate
fresh and whole.

For weeks now, your father and I
have been eating tomatoes as if the harvest's
bounty will never cease. My breasts, too,
are tomato-heavy, the bowl of my belly
dense with the curve that will only continue
to deepen in the months ahead. Lingering
in bed this morning, I lay my hands
along the rise, palms and fingertips
listening for you. *Quickening*,
the doctor called it, the desire
for the coming child. Imagine:
next August, we will carry you
into the garden. We will hold
the fruit to your face;
we will teach you tomatoes.

Aubade

Santa Fe, New Mexico

September, and a dozen ravens
skim the alpine treetops, undulant
as Houdini's cape. Up here
the valley's trammel
gives way to birdsong, wind,
a buzzing fly.
                    In the blue distance,
the Sangre de Cristo mountains,
our sins washed away, for now,
by rivers far older than the tears
Mary shed beneath the cross.
The dog sits in the mesquite tree's
narrow shade, ears cocked,
contemplating sky and the hole
he's digging, his concentration unbroken
by the chartreuse hummingbird
at the hourglass feeder,
its ruby throat a flash of sun
that gives shape to what might seem
an infinite day,
were it not
for the shadows along the flagstones
and the mourning dove, vanishing
but for her fiercely
human cry.

Yellow

Twenty-Nine Weeks

I.

Waking to daybreak's rain,
I'm attuned to the starfish
petals sleeping in the lawn; safflower
stained gold, flowers smaller
even than the unborn hands
of our daughter opening and closing
in this amniotic sea.

Listening to her pedal kicks,
speaking to you, to me,
I think, what a paradoxer yellow is,
hiding itself in sun, as if suddenly shy
before the life-giving mirror.

She swims deep and low;
the signpost navel charts her way
a good four inches beneath. But you,
asleep in the bed next to me, sleep through
these pedal kick first thoughts
of rain and yellow, and the yellow
within my quickening womb;
you do not think (yet) of light
caressing a milk-veined sky.

I think of the color somewhere
between saffron and ochre,
of a golden plover's wing;
how it glows in gray rain light,
but hides in full sun,
bleached out, merging
with pasture, mudflat, stone.

II.

An hour has passed, and still
she turns and counterturns—each
movement a sharp, little trochee—

but she will not, she cannot stand,
until the return of the yellow-
bellied kingbirds who summer here.
Until then I must focus on the spy-
glass yellow of the grackle's eye.

III.

After you wake, we break eggs
into glass and speak of the caramelized
custards that waited behind polished glass
in every Parisian patisserie.
You, too (hand on my belly),
are attuned to her pedal kicks now,
and to the memory of me
pressing my nose to the glass,
enchanted by the yellow slices
on full moon plates, resplendent
in the rain-streaked streets.

Haiku for Autumn

The humble kettle
prays for the spoon—bittersweet,
this taste of copper tears.

Mushroom prayers—wild
rice steamed with walnuts and faith:
comfort in a bowl.

Carrots and parsnips
tumbled in a bin—modest
as divinity.

Teaspoon

Perched along the rim of saucer,
you overhear talk of lovers parting
and reuniting, a child's fever, the soon-
to-be bride's immeasurable dreams.

Cast in silver or in plain steel,
adorned with fleur-de-lis or polished
smooth as glass, you provide the infant
with her first tastes of pureed pear
and the old man with his last.

You do not covet the fork's pronged grasp
nor the cutting prowess of the knife;
not when there remains the promise
of lips curving around your body,
the reassuring clasp of forefinger and thumb,

and then the soapy warmth of the kitchen
sink! As for the clattering
fall to the hardwood floor, this
you count among your greatest feats.

Since containment is your nature,
you imagine yourself a pond in miniature,
all the while relishing the dissolution
that awaits within the steamy swirl of cup.

And once you are packed away
in an attic trunk or left to rust
among a box's clutter, you cling
to the hum of voices and to the tick of clock,
cherishing always
the possibility of your return.

Spirit

Quiet as twilight's willow,
or the pond's ripples
suspended among mirroring trees—

So I imagine those spirits
who linger, not because they are loyal
or restless

but because they cannot
surrender sunlight
refracted within
a spider's web, moss
defining the crevices
of a stone wall,
a tortoiseshell cat
lapping milk
from a china saucer,
pinpoints of vermilion
flashing from
a wild trout's flank.

So I tell myself
when there's one less
biscuit in the breadbox,
when the latch clicks
shut on emptiness,
when I find no explanation
for the gas stove's
lone blue flame. So

by imagining,
by believing in them,
I hope to discover
something more about living.

Generations

Light

My mother remembers little
of my birth, other than the laughing
gas, a vision of my father worrying the hall,
and the time of my arrival—three p.m.

What she cannot forget
is the nurses' refusal to bring me to her.
All of the other babies are bottle-fed.
Raised on a farm in Slovenia, my mother
insisted on her breast.

Pearl

The morning of my first communion,
my mother's mother, Oma, secured my veil
with bobby pins adorned with pearls
she bought especially for the occasion.

In the car afterwards
she unwrapped a jelly Bismarck
and let me eat it
despite the whiteness of my gloves.

Shadow

Two months after the diagnosis,
Oma died of ovarian cancer.
Late May, and I gathered lilacs
by the armful, filling each room
with their perfume,
eager to be surrounded
by the promise of freshly cut grass,
the thrum of bees.

My mother wore sunglasses
for a while after that, weeping
within a silence fragranced by lilacs.

How many years
before she told me
she hardly knew her mother?
I did not ask why, pictured all those years
my mother dreamed
of studying fashion, worked instead
as a downtown architect's
secretary.

In my memory, always, Oma
wears a navy blue dress and matching shoes;
her only adornment, a bit of lace
pinned to her crown.

Lilac

My mother saved the most
beautiful of my baby clothes:
butter-yellow shoes, pink bunting;
and two dresses, both from Oma.

The first is powder blue,
the edges finished with a delicate
ruffle, the bodice a garland
of embroidered flowers.
The other remains purest white
despite the years.

My daughter will be here in January.
My mother was born in late May.
Lilacs always grace her celebration's table.
Only now, touching the stitches
of the white dress, do I realize
I do not know the day
Oma, my grandmother, was born.

Rain's Offering

Rain is not the soft, sighing voice of memory.

It does not seek again the child—
neither her first hesitant steps,
nor her backward glance and wave
the morning she walked down the lane
for the first day of school.

Rain is not tea
steeped in the silence of an English country house,
a hound drowsing beside the fire,
the petals of a rose
falling onto glass.

It cannot chase away the shadows
meandering beneath the birches
nor startle a spider in her web.
And despite the occasional sun shower,
rain remains unfamiliar
with the heat that ripens
the sunflower, freckles
a child's bare arm.

Rain's fingertip cannot divine
the anemone's eyelet heart
nor catch the pulse of galaxies
along a starling's wing.

Rain is a wild-throated thing
that empties itself in the open meadow,
washing away, only to re-imagine
who and where we are.

II

Memories have three epochs.
And the first is like yesterday.

ANNA AKHMATOVA

Little Tesuque

Above Santa Fe, New Mexico

If past and future meet
in a room we step through,
let that room arc into sky.
                 Let the silver
rush of mountain
be lyricized by the loral vireo,
by the secret prayer of owl.
                 Let sun
steep the pine
needles under foot-
steps gentled by stream
violets, white as hope
and five-petaled as the dawn.
                 Let the chaliced
hearts of shepherds' purse
reveal the butterfly's
ruffled gold, the vision
of raven testing
the infinity of sky.

If past and future meet
in an aspen-vaulted room,
                 let the dog cross
the snow-flushed stream
                 fearlessly, let your hand
grasp hold of mine.

Ordinary

Nearing Thirty Weeks

Outside, moon lights the mustard-
seed, hollyhock, pampas grass. Within
the room is candled by a window, needles
and first yarn nesting in a drawer.
                    Across the threshold
into a night small enough to hold both of us
and our daughter—*she's with us always now*—
the dogs following.

Daily we cross the meadow, waiting
for the sun to swallow the horizon.
Through October's ocher, umber,
and the occasional waft of spearmint,
heat lingering. Drift of feedlot,
cottonseed.
                    Rambles lead us back
to a garden drowsy with tomatoes
and the sharpness of thyme. The roses'
leaves crumble between our fingertips.
Still, each week puts forth a new bloom.
                    Hands along my belly,
there, too, ripening—*she is with us*—
I write to her with my palms,
letters bidden not by language,
but by the feel of lambs' ear, soil, moth.

On the doorstep, the neighbor's
white cat—one eye blue, the other gold—
and in the garden by the sagging fence, sun-
flowers sprung from the birdfeeder's leavings.

Skein

Skein of yarn, dawn's mantle,
always you recall tawny pastures
in a country far from my own.
There, the sheep allow themselves
to be shorn. Among grounded stars
they remain, generation after generation,
each stitch a passing year. Gathered close,
they nip the sweet buds of clover,
the taste of earth, of journeys,
ripening on their tongues.

The fluid click of needle, ribbons
of years crossing over as one stitch
joins the next. So the circle grows,
soft and warm enough to cover
a coming daughter's crown.

Is the lure of departure inevitable?
If and when it comes,
who will record the night
they depart the pasture
forsaking the stars, the sweet
drift of clover? And their children—
will they scatter, or remain,
intimate circle of quiet
munching twilight
beneath another heathered sky?

Incomprehensible,
this belief they live on
in stitches I am learning to cast
loosely. So their histories
can breathe, I am learning
not to pull the soft skein tight.

Sky

In this country taut and brown as a finch's wing,
a woman wakes, her sky's worth of fears
gentled in her husband's arms.

How often she feels this,
how often she forgets.

As if such tenderness were a golden bird
too marvelous to behold;
as if the hard, sweet apples on the sideboard
were relics only of the fall.

But just imagine:
that woman waking, her burden turned
into a strong-winged flock.

Through the open window
they rush, lured by the freshening
scent of rain

and she, too, is changed
into one of the dust-colored birds who abide
near glistening rivers, the waters streaming
cold and pure.

Kitchen Haiku in Winter

Silence is plain salt
parsing the fennel seeds, ghosts
asleep in the flour bin.

Silver forks sing
amid sharpened knives—
dangerous pleasures.

Paper whites blossom
on the sill—winter cradled
within verdant sleeves.

Maryam

Yea, a sword shall pierce through thy own soul also

—LUKE 2:34-35

With the others I pray to the Lord, *Yah*
but alone, now, the sheep
tracing the scent of water, it is you, *Nuth*,
to whom I speak. You,
who swallow the sun each night,
birthing it again each dawn.
The lambs, too, are like children,
bleating, nudging, pleading to be carried.

So many years, so many seasons.
I believed I would remain here,
always, a girl and her flock.
This morning Father told me
come winter, I must marry.
Who will tend to the sheep, to the young lambs then?

The oldest ewe, the one born
during my mother's time,
leaves off grazing, nuzzles my arm.
She smells of sun and the lingering musk of sage.
Stumbling over loose stones, I tumble back
to the night I helped deliver her
of a stillborn lamb.

Old as she is—and such a rare gift
the taste of meat—
I lay a pebble on my tongue
and say a prayer, asking you
to preserve her
as the day of the wedding feast draws near.

Preparation

Thirty-Seven Weeks

Pain has no conscience,
no willful intention.
Still, she finds her way
into bobcat and coon dog,
into swallow and dove.
In these weeks before
I will give birth,
pain has found me.
I do not welcome her.
I cannot lay her a place
set with china and silver.
Still, she and I commune.
She does not ask me
to view her as teacher,
or beloved friend, but insists
I accept her burden,
as gift, as vessel
I will labor within,
the rhythms of breath
and beating heart
my primary refuge
as the daughter
within me now—spine
curled against the skull of hip,
unimaginably human
face pressed against
the sciatic nerve's flowering
branches—is delivered,
crying, into this life.

December Prayer

Thirty-Eight Weeks

Bring me the thrush,
its hushed lullaby of song.
Bring me freshly fallen pinecones,
each tree that waits within.
Bring me the cloud's faithfulness
to the sky, the scent of wool,
the brindled light of birches in the rain.
Bring me the first snowfall,
earth's body shimmering silver-white.
Bring me the dusty crystal vase,
its constant promise
of a moment's quiet flowering.
Bring me the deer
who stand at the edge of absence,
the blessing such fleet limbs impart.
Bring me the old horse's fetlocks,
the whistling rhythms
of mallards swimming through
sorrow's dark lake. Bring me
the purple grapes tipped with moonlight,
the windfall apples, the teacup
brimming with my grandmother's tears.
Bring me the hope that abides
within, despite the thin goat
waiting alone in the clearing,
despite my stubborn heart.

Bring me all of these,
then one by one, I ask you
to take them away, and bring me
only your night's secrets,
the cupboard housing
your bone-white fears.

Bring them to me.
I will wash them gently. I will
set them in the sun to dry.

Hand in hand, we will step forth
into the heron light of morning.
Hand in hand, we will bow down
and greet another dawn.

Poised

Thirty-Nine Weeks

At the back gate, a covey
of inca doves, and the courteous dog,
prick ears cocked, poised for a visitor.

This morning feels gentle
as the hand that cups the fallen fledgling,
as the kiss that calms the startled child.

Laddered between anything is possible
and *the unforeseen*, patience
is the cardinal seen through deep snow.

Or perhaps it is the Indian pony
swishing its tail in twilight's pasture.
At its feet, a thousand seedlings
await their chance to bloom.

And within my womb, you, too, are waiting.
Not quite January, and already
I am twining April's leaf-flocked
flowers through your hair.

Surrender

Is the breath of child
birth, oblivion's guttural
clutch, followed by
the blue sage, deliverance,
the moment the ear listens
to her heart held
within your palm

Render the persimmon
range of hummingbird,
emerald heights burnished by sun

Render the memory
of snow echoed in a fawn's
passage through lupine
fields at dawn

Then, hear, if you can,
the spider silkening her web

And try to remember
Indian firewheel and evening
primrose, nourishment
for a clan of snow shoe
rabbits, and the woman,
not quite a stranger,
who abided here
once, alone.

Rereading *The Velveteen Rabbit*

Just two days until Christmas,
and our first fir tree perfumes the air.
Adorned with bracelets of colored light
and a single seam of white twined around
its middle, I cannot look at that tree
without thinking of you. Even the snow
on the neighboring rooftops, the pulse
of ice falling from the eaves—
are made new by your coming.

This morning, curled beneath the afghan,
the dog a stout parcel beside me,
I read *The Velveteen Rabbit*, imagining
the day I would read the story to you.

What is Real? asked the Rabbit.

You become. It takes a long time.

How often I've been told
mine is an old soul, vessel
or star-streaked planet bearing
echoes of other lives. Always
I believed this, though it's only now
I understand how much more Real
my life's become because I carry you,
whose face I cannot yet capture,
whose petal fingers will curl around my own.

In this ninth month, even the memory
of my body before you has grown thin
as the velveteen of the Rabbit's hide.

Still, I know I once walked through a day
without you.

When a child loves you...then you become Real.

A constant becoming
real as your rhythmic paddling.

Head down, held by my pelvis,
this *lightening* is the sign of your coming,
your becoming. How many times,
braced against December's cold,
have I conjured the moment when
they will place you in my arms,
umbilical cord, that life-line joining us
since the beginning, about to be severed,
your coming defined by hospital lights
and by faces I, too, do not yet know.

> *Does it hurt? asked the Rabbit.*

Never again will the days—
yours and mine—be so self-contained.
Even now, my breath moves
inside you, my unborn child,
unfamiliar still with wind and cold,
but also with the caress of lip,
the touch of hand.

> *Does it hurt?*

How soon before they lay you
close to my heart bearing traces
of the journey I cannot imagine,
no matter how often I try, the truth
of your coming as unreal to me still
as the hind legs the Velveteen Rabbit
finds turned to flesh and blood,
the legs he comes to recognize.

As I will recognize you.

III

There in the distance, bonneted,
round as the hairline of a child—
indefinite and infinite with hope—

EAVAN BOLAND

Daughter, Here

is the morning's fountain serenading three flame-gold fish
feathering the purpurine depths of the pool.

Here are lily pads and tripping crane flies and a circle of mossy stones.

Here is the apricot-bellied phoebe whistling to her mate, there
the vermilion flycatcher who dips and rises within the rolling
       heights of song.

Here are cinnabar ladies' tresses, early iris, and columbine's fluted
       gold.
Here pewter lambs ear, emblem of childhood's most ardent hope;
       even scarlet creeper, twining around trellis and
       abandoned chair.
Here dusky lavender and ethereal lemon balm, there peppermint
       and hardy marjoram.

Now the jaguar disguised as housecat arrives, charcoal fur thatched
       with burr and soil.
Traipsing across fence posts, she spies aureate eyes glowing through
       an imagined jungle's deepest green.

Here are tasseled heads of garlic, each papery orb concealing
       the pungent witchery of gardens. Here
returning sweet peas planted from seed, and buried far beneath,
       one of the dog's forgotten bones.

Here is snowmelt turned to starflower and spider web shimmering
       in sun.
Here is the dust of ancestors and the dandelion's fairest wish. Here is
       rabbit hole, vole's hollow, even the raven's merlin glow.

Here is the phoebe returned to her nest secreted high in the eaves,
       there the child who crouches over sun-drenched stones
       in search of centipede.

Now an etiolate sliver of moon hums a lullaby to the retiring sun.
Now the circle of stones releases the heat they have basked in all day.

When the stars nestle into the branches, they, too, will listen
    to the chur of cricket, and to the fountain still

serenading three flame-gold fish feathering the purpurine depths
    of the pool.

Triolet

Yellow crocuses on white snow;
Moonglow, a chalice of sun to hold
Up to winter. My daughter's toes:
Yellow crocuses on white snow.
Icicles for breakfast, even the air knows
Nazareth awaits, more precious than gold.
Yellow crocuses on white snow:
Moonglow—a chalice of sun to hold.

Crumpets, Old-Fashioned Fare

The batter requires attacking with vivacious turbulence
—WALTER BANFIELD, Manna, 1937

Enticing as laughter, who would not love a crumpet,
Honey-combed cake griddled in tin and served hot with butter?
Children, as the old saying goes, are fondest of crumpets.

It's breakfast time for child, clown, and bear. *Tea!* trumpets
My daughter, as dog and cat arrive to inspect the platter.
More beloved than a pikelet, who would not love a crumpet?

Along with good judgment, patience is required for crumpets—
Patience and home-milled flour.
Children, in denim or lace, are fondest of crumpets.

Not to be confused with the spongy muffin (a French import),
A testament to the crumpet are the crumbs sprinkling my daughter's
Cheeks, surrounding her chair. So tempting, jam and crumpets

Served hearthside, on sturdy crockery, thumbprints
Buttering the glass, and for accompaniment—the rain's pitter patter.
Children, our grandparents knew, are fondest of crumpets.

Today bread is uniform, and crumpet-making, a battered art.
On street-corners, children gobble Twinkies in plastic wrappers.
Yeast-leavened as laughter, who would not master the crumpet
When children, as the old saying goes, are fondest of crumpets?

Edible Light

A Compilation of Children's Verse

Day by day and night by night, she sailed
away for a year and a day
while the pattering rain drove by.

Quick little splinter, she danced
by the light of the moon,
pearled with dew like fishes' eyes.

And because she loved secrets
she believed a noiseless patient spider:
alone, important, wise.

All the week she hid from sight,
gathering treasures of edible light
in a beautiful, pea-green boat.

And the yellow pears dropped
day and night, and night and day
surrounded by the turquoise sea.

Close to the sun in lonely lands,
waves big as glassy mountains:
visible, invisible, fluctuating charms.

The moon spun round like a top.
A black crow flew over,
lifting his delicate feet.

With only the spiders sailing their webs,
she sailed away for a year and a day:
quick little splinter.

Until she went in on tiptoe.

Locomotion

For the record: you learned to crawl
in Paris, pink palms slapping
the tile, rump tilted high in the air,

petal knees scooting. *Grab Sophie!*
Grab her—fast! It was fall—
pear-gold October—and you crawled

after amber leaves, ruddy squirrels. You
crawled beneath tables and chairs, slapping
your palms together, laughing. *Stop, Sophie!*

Ever-alert, I stopped countless air-
borne free falls (but not all). Air—
how I longed to give it form when first you fell

head-first on the concrete. *Kiss Sophie's
forehead! Her knees!* New to walking, crawling,
once so perilous, smack-slapped

of safety—of limits at least. Now that you
could walk—*Where is she? Where's Sophie?*—you
swayed, tipped, tumbled, kissed air

only to try again. And again. We slapped
on ladybug shoes and a cushy diaper, and falls
no longer daunted. Yes, you still crawled

for comfort's sake (sometimes). *Look at Sophie!*
we'd coo, nostalgic, forlorn. *Sophie,*
our baby, where has she gone? This morning finds you

twirling in circles! How long since the air
tasted of frost, and we buttoned up our coats?
Slap! and my lagging eye catches up with the slap-

snap of calendar. Today it's crocuses, Sophie.
Tomorrow—daffodils. Learn to rejoice in falling,
in transformation's free fall. Winter, you're

learning, must reign, before the air
brings forth bumblebees and blossoms.
Crawling? Just the beginning, Sophia.

Word Play

Words lead to, words love, words lure worlds... World, from *weoruld, wuruld, worold*—world: this present life. The Owl and the Pussy-Cat went to sea in a beautiful pea-green boat. Not verdigris, teal, or aquamarine, but pea-green—each a tiny sphere, a word-world. Words lure worlds. In the cowslip pips I lie, hidden from a buzzing fly. Pip—the small seed of a fruit. Apple, pear, pomegranate. Pip—the sound a chick makes. So many words, so many worlds. Serendipitous, scintillate, splendiferous. Words, they turn buoyant, balloon skyward, they blossom in your mouth, a petal-light daisy chain taking flight. Daisies and balloons. Pip-pip-pip. Words, you're learning, can be kitten-quick, puddle-duck playful, lazy as lizards lounging in the sun. Iguana or chameleon? Crocodile or fish? A fish is not a lizard. Why then the lizard fish, that large-mouthed bottom dweller in the pea-green sea? Not verdigris, teal, or aquamarine, but pea-green like the Owl and the Pussy-Cat's boat.

They took some honey...Clover, buckwheat, or wildflower? In the cowslip pips I lie. Cowslip honey? Visible, invisible, fluctuating charms. Words lead to, words love, words lure worlds. My sweet daddy, my mommy, Mommy mine. Sweet is to Daddy as Honey is to Mommy is to Mine. But words are not always bouquets, offerings, tributes, a moonlit walk beside the sea. Some words bite. Naughty! Bad! Don't hit—we don't hit! No! So the honey jar topples, tumbles, falls from the cupboard shelf, sticky glass shattering everywhere. What a mess! Look at the mess you've made! How doth the little crocodile? Words, you're learning, can snap—can open up an underworld of tears. Then words lose, words languish, words lie among the sharp-toothed, the tarantula-fierce....So they sailed away for a year and a day, sailed the pea-green sea in a pea-green boat, their honeyed provisions (miraculously) replenishing themselves day by day.

Once you knew a wordless world, the womb world of rhythm-pulse-heartbeat—visible, invisible—its own fluctuating charm. But to try (impossible!) to recover the pre-verbal sea would mean losing the light of moon rhymes with spoon rhymes with baboon turned to a balloon come to carry us away. When the Owl and the Pussy-Cat dined, it was on mince and slices of quince, served with a runcible spoon. What happened to the honey? High on the cupboard shelf, amber-gold, topaz precious, a flask of bottled sun. Words love, words lure, words lead to worlds: temptresses and angels, whispers and charms. Visible, invisible. Word by word, day by day, a tapestry of A, B, C, a school of quick, bright fish swimming in a rainbow-sequined sea we word smiths, word-mongers, word lovers, we wordlings trawl daily. So words lead to worlds. Visible, invisible, fluctuating charms loved by bottom-dweller and monarch butterfly, by lizard-fish and angel, by pomegranate and pear. So words lure worlds into this present life.

Wings

The toddler in pink tulle, my daughter, is growing wings.
Feathers? You're telling me she's sprouting feathers?
Not feathers—wings. Catch me, Mommy, she sings,

Leaping into my arms one minute, flinging
Herself away the next. How do you tether a toddler?
That toddler in pink tulle, my daughter, the one growing wings.

There's a tradition of clipping a bird's wings. You're kidding?
To ground a miniature sun, keep her from soaring—it's against nature.
Not feathers—wings. Catch me, Mommy, she sings,

Delighting in dizzying leaps from swing and armchair.
The rose finch wakes, the robin, and she's out in the weather.
The toddler in pink tulle, my daughter, is growing wings.

Sometimes her scraping heights terrify. Jumping, spiraling
Into air. Such limits: Impossible to measure.
Not feathers—wings. Catch me, Mommy, she sings.

Airplane! Bird! Away she dashes, any bright, winged thing
Compels her to try new territories—new skies of pleasure.
The toddler in pink tulle, my daughter, is growing wings.
Not feathers. Wings catch me, Mommy, she sings.

Rufous Hummingbird

Liquid copper,
pulse of sun, you
iridesce from fairy

slipper to globe
flower, graze the tooth
of a shooting star

Hope unfettered,
you're thinned
to feathers

the force
of light held
in a penny

netting scarlet
trumpets
you lattice the air

Just Two

Dressed in periwinkle blue
velvet, white tights, pewter shoes,
you cry, *Church-going, Daddy and I
go Church*. Laughing, you let me
brush your meadowlark hair. Bunny—*my
bunny*, you tell bunny, snug in dimpled arms.
Twenty pounds, feather or stone? In my arms

I hold you still. *Song, Mommy!* Blue
songs, sad songs—*que sera, sera*—my
primary repertoire, this crushed velvet, shoe-
less routine, morning and night, you and I
follow, mother and daughter. You're two,
and still I return to the hour of your birth, the first
hour I nursed you. I nurse you still. Snug
in my arms, your periwinkle blue eyes provoke me
into a giggling tilt-a-whirl, the antithesis of blue.

Just two, you insist on shoes—
Shoes and socks, Mommy—for bed, my
Capricorn-bright child, my radish rose, my
two year old terror, my love. Already I
believe I see the long-limbed girl, shoes
scuffed from a day's playing out of my arms'
reach. Growing up, you are. Blue
I will not be. Not me,
a mother—yours—what belongs to me:

you. This morning every drawer in my
kitchen lies helter-skelter. You are blue-
berry lipped, blue-berry fingered. *I
eat, Mommy. Hold, Mommy*. In my arms
I will hold you, until your shoes
skim my knees. Walk in my shoes.
You literally do. Tilt-a-whirl girl. *Me.*

Watch me, Mommy! Into my arms
you run, crying, *My mommy, my*
daddy, my bunny. Mine. I
want to give you the world, mottled blue
oyster, ocean gemstone, shoe-
shined, jewel-toned. Listen to me.
I promise. For now, just sleep in my arms.

Two Happinesses

Take this afternoon's silver-gray light
of maple branching towards evening;
our cat, ink-dark, skittering across the grass.
Somewhere deep within the winter-sleep of yards,
a dog barks. And within the mirror's triptych,
the flickering of advent candle,
green stemmed narcissus rising from a glass.

And at the same time, I'm leaving
a trail of breadcrumbs along a cobbled street
near the Musée Rodin; in my basket,
the remains of a seed-flecked baguette,
an untouched round of cheese, purple grapes.

Two happinesses coming together, two comforts.
Like the childhood shine of my grandmother's
amethyst worn beside this rose gold wedding ring.
Just now, the light beyond the windows
is blue as the stained glass of Chartres,
cathedral I haven't seen in fifteen years.

Still the prayers of the white tapers.
Still the ascent of pigeons, higher, higher,
until they seem one with the belfry's rafters.
Still a glass so impossibly blue as to silence
the sands of the centuries' hourglass.

Valentine

My silver teaspoon, Daddy's cozy mouse,
Not hand-me-downs but heirlooms,
So too, my baptismal cross,
Shelves full of Once Upon a Time.

Not hand-me-downs but heirlooms:
Threads of folksong,
Shelves full of Once Upon a Time,
Grandma's cache of photographs.

Threads of folksong,
Grandpapa's stories and questions,
Grandma's cache of photographs,
Ribbon salvaged by the doves.

Grandpapa's stories and questions;
These, I ask you to cherish;
Ribbon salvaged by the doves,
The tennis ball Eddie guards in the yard.

These I ask you to cherish:
A porcelain tea set from Limoges,
The tennis ball Eddie guards in the yard,
But what of my moon-shaped fears?

A porcelain tea set from Limoges:
So many gifts for you, bluebird.
But what of my moon-shaped fears?
Are my shadows to be yours, too?

So many gifts for you, bluebird:
A pumpkin hat, frayed finger puppets.
Are my shadows to be yours, too?
Are there hours enough to contain these years?

A pumpkin hat, frayed finger puppets,
My baptismal cross.
Give me years enough to embrace these hours,
My silver teaspoon, Daddy's cozy mouse.

Waiting Room, Fever

I.

Diapers, baby wipes, biscotti
and picture books: I came prepared
and feverish (103).
                    Nurse, Mommy! Nurse!
You tug my shirt—and a smile—
moonlit, knowing, flickers
across the nearby 6'7" basketball player's face.
Nurse, Mommy!
                    How about a cookie?
Mommy, I want nurse!
                    You're two. I thought
I'd have you weaned by now
            Nurse!
but for the comfort of that quiet country
you and I alone occupy
                    Mommy, Nurse!

II.

Wheel-chair bound, head like a neglected flower,
the boy beside us looks about twelve.
His pigeon-toed feet are sneaker-clad.
Sneakers for a boy who will never kick a soccer ball,
lope across a meadow, run for a bus—
                    Baby!
No, Bunny, he's a boy, and he doesn't feel well.
Your eyes, blue as my own, meet mine—do you
understand?
                    Baby, Mommy!

The boy's mother swabs his brow.
She looks English and old-fashioned.
With her red hair flipped up like Doris Day,
she should be wearing a silky floral dress, pearls.

But she must lift him
into bed, the car, onto the toilet—the reason,
I presume, for her jeans
and orthopedic shoes.

The wheelchair is heavy.
The boy must weigh seventy-five pounds.
Once she carried him in her womb.

III.

At last, in the exam room's fluorescent glare,
I lift you to my breast.
The nurse sticks a thermometer in my ear,
swabs my nose.
                    You're in school? she asks.
I'm a teacher.
                    Oh, honey.
Such knowledge of the way things are
in that honey-coated word, I think,
returned to that boy and his mother waiting, still, beyond—.

Returned, too, to those Sunday mornings
when I sat in the church pew beside my mother.
Always, a few rows ahead, an elderly father
and his middle-aged son.
He wore thick glasses and spoke like a child.
His father held his hand after Communion.
They loved each other.
As a child, I knew this.

IV.

Driving home, a pale sun breaks through the rain.
At the stoplight, I turn to you,
reach out to stroke your cheek.
It's okay, Mommy, you say. *It's okay.*

Firefly

After days of rain, the blue
jay's wing is reborn as sky.
His black eye finds the earth
worm burrowed deep
into a tomorrow
unknowable as the swallowtail
butterfly's wing
beneath which I sleep,
sheltered, as I would shelter
my mother's ginger-root hands.

Years ago
she opened those hands,
smooth as willow then,
and beckoned night's fireflies,
trusting these winged lanterns
to carry prayers
to her own mother, all
she could not speak aloud.

And even now she speaks to me of fireflies—.

Black as the hiding soul,
the swallowtail's wing
haloes its mysteries
in yellow, tiny moons,
six of them:

six fireflies that return to me

you, mother.

Art Lesson: Julie Manet Walks with Renoir

I.

Black and white are not colors. There is no black in nature.
Black happens when an object absorbs all the wavelengths.
Consider Monet's *Gare Saint Lazare*, the pitch dark locomotives

created from vermilion, ultramarine, emerald.
Consider alders and blackberries, ashes and shadows.
Shadows are not black. No shadow is black.

A shadow is a veil. In darkness or deep shade,
the veil is thick. In bright light, the veil is thin.
Black is a hoarding of light; its utter refusal, white.

II.

So Renoir explains, pausing
every now and again to observe
the sunlight suspended in the leaves;

or a butterfly's velvet dark,
more violet than black
against the bright head of marigold.

Since her mother's death,
when Julie woke to December
sunshine and the surprise of

just-fallen snow enfolding
the new sky's greens and yellows,
Julie has come to see

black and white as absolutes.
The morning light left her
mother's eyes, black

became absence. But white—
Julie envisions the lavender
reflection of light on snow,

light like those childhood
mornings she and her mother drew
copper teapots, peaches

ripening in sun, the blackbird's
glossy wing. *White* became
the glimmer on a silver jar,

the sheen of a pomegranate
seed, a baby's tooth,
the inner life of pearl.

No, my dear, Renoir says gently.
White reflects light away from it.
White absorbs almost no light.

White has a black heart.
Julie listens, for she loves Renoir
and his smiling, happy pictures.

Julie loves Renoir, though she prefers
Degas and his obsessions;
and admires above all Manet,

her father's brother, and the great
love, the only love, of her mother's life.
(Why Julie cannot like him.)

But Manet's art...*Berthe Morisot*
with a Bouquet of Violets.
Swathed in black lace,

her mother sits, luminous and
blue as the Magdalene,
though Manet painted her mother's

eyes black, not their actual green,
like cut jade, that secret color,
suggestive of gardens.

Renoir gestures towards a bed
of yellow poppies. Yellow, the light
of nature, her mother believed,

teaching her to distinguish
between turmeric and marigold,
mango and saffron.

So many yellows. Julie loves
the earthy amber most, its ancient
sense of land as a living being

returning her to the wild place
she and her mother visited
that last August before she,

and then her mother, became ill.
Wandering away from the sunlit meadow,
they entered the forest—

a shadow is a veil.
There violets bloomed beside ochre-
capped mushrooms. Violet, the last

color in the rainbow spectrum.
Violet, where the known ends,
and the unknown begins.

Is it true, Julie asks Renoir now,
bending to examine the butterfly,
surprised by hints of crimson

along the wing—*how easily reds fade*—
that butterflies can see purple but not red?
Funny girl, what makes you think of that?

I read it somewhere. In a scientific journal.
I don't know.
I don't have an answer.

Shadows always have a color.
A shadow is a veil.
Julie smiles.

She clasps Renoir's hand more tightly.
She listens more carefully.
She believes it must be true,

just as she believes violet
to be the last color of the rainbow,
a belief that brings her mother,

dressed in Manet's violet blacks,
the bouquet of violets
pinned to her bodice, becoming

neither intimate or familiar,
but just near enough
for a daughter to beckon.

IV

And the end of all our exploring
Will be to arrive where we started
And know the place for the first time.

T.S. ELIOT

Mi Se

from the Chinese, meaning "mysterious color"

Light carved from the mountain, light that dyes
the river green, I do not seek you
among excavated tombs, or within
the chambers of ruined towers,
foreign graves.

Those without speech know
such light lichens the hawthorn's
branches, deepens the forest floor with angel
fern, moss willow, thyme.

Such light crazes porcelain's glaze,
compels the woman quick with child
to greet the dawn. Its rule is prophecy,
and its relics, perplexing
only if one believes it born
from a mythic man's fall.

Better to believe such light
is the perfect pigment, *Mi Se*,
transposed into sadness, waves,
the souls of gardens. Believe the sky
dreams within light's orbit
beyond a Palladian window veined
with leaves so intricately formed
they recall the small, wild trout
that swim through mountain streams
ferrying with them
all the wishes of our surrendered years.

Jonquils

—from Narcissus, ναρκάω *narkao,*
"to grow numb" in Greek

Is it possible to know someone
even if you share night's same bed—
his warm hand on your shoulder
nudging you out of a dream
in which your first love appears
younger than you are now,
younger than you believed you ever were.

Just over there, just out of reach,
in the corner of a garden
you can almost remember—
the sweet, heavy scent of jonquils—
the two or three live oaks
extending their rustling lattice
over a bench where he sits
waiting. Such astonishing light,
as in the paintings of the Old Masters,
all gold leaf and shadow, and inviting
as the Vermeer-blue pitcher
your grandmother—
her eyes just that blue—
kept on the sideboard. Sometimes
she filled that pitcher
with the jonquils from her garden
the wild rabbits ate at nightfall,
their small whiskers twitching in the dark.

So many years ago, that garden.
Still your fingertips remember
the skin of the petals, and the cracked
leather of her album, the one she carried

across spot-lit borders. (Your own father lost
his stuffed bear on one such crossing,
and your grandfather cupped a hand
over his mouth to hush his crying.)
The album remains,
preserved in plastic on some high shelf
in your sleepless father's house.

Nothing remains of her brother,
the one who died during the war,
younger, then, than your first lover
and just as beautiful. *Misha, Mishinka*—
she called to him
all through those last afternoons
she sat beside the window
looking out at her garden, too tired
and yes, too far away to fret over the rabbits.

Just once she scolded the boy you loved.
His overcoat was majestic, she said,
and yours was shabby.
You were engaged by then,
two children really, playing house
in turn-of-the-century rooms at university.
Your grandmother knew this boy,
his blue eyes, the wheat blonde of his hair
like the blonde of a Russian boy
she loved once. This boy,
but not the one who sleeps beside you
now, whose favorite flower you do not know,
though you want to believe they're jonquils.

Heights

The green swing held a boy two years too big
for its swoop of plastic, his sock feet pecking the ground
beneath the frayed hem of his jeans. Ten, maybe eleven,
he watched my daughter push her doll on the neighboring swing.
Where are your shoes? I asked him, as dusk gave way to night,
and a clamor of geese spooled the silhouette of pond.
Where are your shoes? His mouth stumbled into a shape
that would not shape words; his hands fluttered in his lap,
paired birds but flightless. *Where is your mother?*
Stupid question, since I now knew he could not answer.
What I also knew—that he wanted someone to push his swing
into the shiver of pink ribboning the almost-dark sky,
and that someone was me. Why, then, did I turn
towards the glint of windows
in the distance? While above us, the air filled
with still more geese, a prayer chain of dark against light,
an eternal murmuring of wings, of flight. My child
climbed into the swing, and the boy's eyes followed
the pump-pump of her small legs tilting up into sky.
And I didn't even push his swing. When the boy's
mother and a man appeared—from where?
where had they gone?—her eyes, like the boy's,
held the dark. It was the man, alone, tattooed arms
bared to the cold, who pushed the boy, hard and fast,
until laughter sputtered out of the place in this child
where speech should have lived. The man turned away, then,
to kiss the woman. The swing slowed,
and my chatterbox daughter quieted,
attentive to the boy's sock feet dragging the ground.
The air had turned chilly. It was time
to leave. We left him there, this boy,
his mother and the man continuing to kiss, the geese
on the water, having settled in for the night.

Plain Air

You made your home in my hand
learning to balance
within my finger spaces, learning
song, milk, sleep
the blue freedom
of sheltered flight

Above our hemisphere
the un-tethered sanctuary
of birds, a testament
I believed
to our solitary orbit

How could I forget
lives, like years
hurry ahead
branching, limbing
territories further than
the sheltered hand

No, you say
the birds build nests in our trees
the birds are the same
they remain

I could tell you about the birds
and their migrations
I could tell you
the birds will forget
we were here

Abide with Me

The neighborhood gun shop squats beside Daybreak Donuts,
and on the other side, *Gifts of Genuine Leather*
blinks in pink neon. Above the morning traffic
a billboard frames a congressman posing in camouflage
beside his sons. Each holds a rifle in his hands.
                                        Jogging past
in the frail hour after dawn, I breathe in the doughy sweetness,
brooding over yesterday's gospel: Jesus's forty days
in the wilderness, Satan singing in his ear.

"Do not put your God to the test," Jesus tells the Devil
though already he could hear the voices chanting,
                                        "Crucify him, crucify him."
According to Luke, Satan departs until *an opportune time.*

What about Mary?
Was her Son's promise of salvation enough
to see her through a wilderness vaster than his own?

On the way back, I pass Daybreak Donuts.
A woman from the supermarket sits on the stoop, smokes.
Grease seeps through the paper bag at her side.
Before her son O.D'd, she taught fourth grade. Now
she works the nightshift, bagging oranges and beer.

I look away, meet the eyes
of the ruddy-faced congressman
still grinning overhead,
November's air burdened by sugar, ash, gasoline.

Harvest

Haven of shade in high summer, this late the white oak
wearies with her ceaseless relinquishing of leaves. Today
I rake still more leaves, trying to convince myself
of the tai-chi of leaf raking in the bourbon light of late afternoon,
a dowager's tea hour, an hour in which to mend things, or sleep.
My daughter plays among the mums and ornamental cabbages,
calling out nursery rhymes, snatches of song, the occasional
sailor's oath—her inheritance from me.
        Up north
my mother fades beneath the gray rain of November.
Always she tries to hurry ahead
into the clean slate of snow and trees silhouetted
against pristine sky. Why?—
when her own mother filled her pockets with promise,
even those months she knew she was dying.
Gentle and silent, to my child's mind, my grandmother's eyes,
luminous and raven-dark, harbored the mystery
of acorns and seeds.

Come jump in the leaves, I call to my daughter, straying again,
this time as far as the neighbor's yard. I stoop
to scoop up another armful, and my hands greet a chill weight,
a scrape of claw. Here are the cindered eyes of a squirrel,
its decay delayed by leaf shroud, by shade. *It's dead, Mama.*
My daughter is matter-of-fact, a sturdy child in boots and sweater.
I search for something, some offering,
wishing she had not seen the squirrel—why hurry this?
        But she is off again,
spiraling into leaves. *Look, Mama*, she cries,
light, delighted, burrowing deep. *Look, I'm making a nest.*

Catechumens

Why did I wake today
to Mary's face, blue-veiled,

in shadow,
a thousand, tiny flames peeping at her feet?

Ash Wednesday, yes of course, I remember,
and my grandmother has been dead for seven years.

She grew peonies, heavy-headed blooms
of white and pink and plum-tipped scarlet.

Summer nights before bed
we laid the table for breakfast:

fresh strawberries, corn flakes, real cream;
everything in her kitchen neatly labeled, clean.

Some days I wake wishing
I could seize hold of her blue-veined hand

and become that child again,
the ballerina in her south side salon

who helped in her search
for lily pads and wild mushrooms.

I want to share that child's secrets—

but I can't catch her,
and these days, testing her freedom,

my daughter
runs away when I call.

Yesterday, a stray dog, gray-furred,
darted in and out of traffic.

The cars came fast.
I swerved away just in time.

This is how it is, I thought.
We are anointed with ashes and tears.

But today, Ash Wednesday,
the light is limned with gold,

the ramshackle house down the road
wears a coat of fresh red paint,

and someone is playing the trumpet.
Even the cherry laurel I thought we'd lost,

roots torn up by ice,
is standing upright again,

propped by wooden planks,
roots rejoined to soil.

We are nearly two months away
from the shortest day of the year,

my mother tells me over the phone.
Foot-long icicles shear her windows,

my father shovels still more snow,
and inside she bakes bread and plans

her garden, anticipating the purple fragrance
of lilacs that will surround the house

and the Easter hyacinths and blue bells
she will bring to the cemetery

to plant on her mother's grave.
We must learn to re-invent our happiness

is what she tells me.
This is how it is.

Little Notes of Grace

A light exists in Spring...
It passes and we stay....

—EMILY DICKINSON

These light-filled lines return
as you and I, Daughter, walk through
May's twilight, flushed by a hundred
robins chorusing in the elms.
To think I almost overlook
their little notes of grace,
preoccupied with the latest migrants—
a trio of vultures roosting
in our ninety-eight-year-old neighbor's oak—
and the quarrels with your father.

It passes and we stay,
the light and the quarrels,
though the notes remain, burrowed
in the soil like the gray-white larvae
the robins eat; burrowing, too, into my dreams
until I wake, dreams of lost
dogs, of ponies trapped in mines,
pulsing behind my lids.
Why I'm grateful the robins
will remain long after
the lengthening days of May
give way to summer's glare—
how quickly, too quickly it passes,
quick as the overnight crocuses.

Why do shadows copy us? you ask,
When will Grandma die?...When I'm
all grown up?...Why?

So many questions, some blue
as robins' eggs, or forget-me-
nots in full sun; others secret as
the soil secreting the memory
of that first robin I buried
some thirty-years ago, my shovel
a teaspoon, a mound of violets
freshening that first grave. *Mama!*
I asked you why…

Oh Daughter, please,
for now just listen
to the robins in the trees;
listen to their voices rise
and fall, and look at the silver
sheen along the branches.
The truth is, I know so little;
and you, my darling, cannot
accept my lack of answers.

One Happiness, or Solange

There is only one happiness in life, to love and be loved
—GEORGE SAND

Among the chestnut and pied plane trees,
the chaffinches are singing. Only
Solange, walking with agitated step

up and down the gravel paths,
is not buoyed by their presence.
Neither by the chaffinches

nor by the dusky wrens, flag tails
held high. No, not even the tangerine-
breasted robins can cheer her.

Solange once held just such a thrush
in the bowl of her hands,
a thrush she found in the boudoir

overlooking the garden
of her father's house. Crammed
with books and her mother's

collection of rocks, butterflies,
and a cricket named Cri-cri,
this room reserved for her

mother's writing compelled Solange,
forbidden entry there.
The thrush lay on the desk

beside the sealing wax and ink,
its body still warm. Had it flown
through the open window?

Or had her mother carried it back
from the garden, its heart still
beating against her palm?

*

Moments, Solange recalls the bird—
rainy mornings when she stares
at the glazed streets; soft-spined

afternoons, grisaille light
tessellating the windowpanes;
nights the neighbor's piano

drifts through the floorboards
when she's alone. Even here
among these paths she first explored

as a child, the thrush returns.
But not today. Today belongs
only to Jeanne-Gabrielle, *Nini*,

her daughter, born and lost
in a room far from the sculptor-
husband, husband-drunkard,

her scribbling mother chose.
My mother, my enemy,
Solange told Chopin, beloved

confidante, beloved friend,
who spoke to her of Shakespeare,
and so transformed this garden

into a fairyland where Solange,
not her mother, reigned as queen.
Chopin alone gave her mother

word of the baby girl's birth and death.
That chance meeting in a stairwell.
Mother's face? What she said?

Solange dared not ask.
In trying to picture her mother, Solange
recovers only the song-less thrush.

*

New Year's Day, and nine-year-old
Solange waited, the basket
she'd prepared spoiling in a corner.

I haven't forgotten you, Mama.
A child's tentative script on paper.
I give you a thousand kisses.

Still her mother did not come.
But the child, Jeanne-Gabrielle.
What if *my* child had lived?

Solange asks, lingering
beside la Fóntaine Medicis,
subtle waters murmuring sounds

deep as thought. How vividly
she pictured them here
beside the fountain, her daughter

safe in her lap. Together
they could have followed a wren's
progress through a thatch of green.

With Jeanne-Gabrielle,
it could have been different.
Or so Solange told herself

when the nurse nestled the infant
in her arms, a child so small
she could have fit in any one

of the many drawers housing
her grandmother's collection.

Candela

Not the flame
of blue illuminating
midnight's kitchen.

Nor the ice-lit stars
brooding
over winter's
seed-dark fields.

Rather, a guide,
one whose name remains
Godes candel—within your eye
those who seek
can always find the sun.

Discreet as first light,
you know how to hide
the diminishment of a room
once lined with sable
curtains, polished glass.

Gentle as dusk's pasture,
within you
even the humblest apple,
the roughest chair,
are turned to gold leaf.

Through you,
the recognizable becomes
newly strange, and the foreign,
more wholly, more
intimately known.

How then to explain,
if tipped by the cat,
or blown by wind hurrying in
through the open window,
you set all that surrounds
to perishing?

Shelter

Through the chain link fence,
the brindle-coated Kara's eyes
yearn toward mine. Between Kara
and Mr. Brown, her escape artist brother,
is Winnie, the incontinent yellow lab
who bellows at my approach, her
baritone cry deepening as I ease through
the metal gate and enter the pen
holding Lucy, another lab, but paler,
butter-colored, and so shy
it takes several minutes to collar her.
                        Like an old lady
baffled at her arrival in a nursing home
and the loss of everything familiar—the bed
in which she slept all her life, the sunny spot
before a living room window—
Lucy lays no claim to the name
she's been given here. And why should she
allow me to lead her away from Kara
and the chorusing others, as if decibels
could sway my choice, so that all I hear is
Choose me! Choose me!

My daughter, now four, waits on the other side.
I'll hold the leash, she tells me, amid
the cacophony of others. *My turn, Mommy.*
                          Later
driving home through the blanched fields
of early March, surrounded by scabbed earth
pocked with old tires and rusting farm machinery,
I will ask myself if it's better, somehow,
to know so little
of this life into which I've brought her.
How much do the dogs know?

Which doggie do you like? I ask Sophie,
the absurdity of the question equaled by my own
free-falling need to bring Lucy and
the mixed breed home—and what of Kara?
The Galilean sea of her eyes?

Well, Soph? I ask again.
The purple one, Mommy, she says. And then:
Can we come back tomorrow?

Soliloquy in Blue

For the robins in the elm and locust trees
I encourage the earth
                        worms, blind
and toothless prophets.

To promote the wren
                        and concede the starling
I offer
                        a pristine bath
among loosestrife and iris.

            Sometimes red is desirable—

why not welcome that luxuriant queen,
      the American beauty?
                      Or the lone cardinal's
promise come November?
                  Yellow (generally)
consecrates the dawn. Blue's

           the scent of monsoon,

the body's fraying shawl of hours.

           How, then, to explain
that trinity of robin's eggs,

                  rush of damselfly,

migrant glory of morning
             twining around sagging fence
or rogue wood pile?

Blue alone
repeats moonlight, the silver-
throated sheen of frog song
on midnight's pond water.

Look, the salamanders have gone.

Come dusk, the bird bath
(save a few water-logged feathers)
will be empty.

Time, then, to embrace this sister
to infinity,
her thrush song

so unlike the cry
of mockingbird
buffeting

all we cannot know
of those cherished rooms,

hushed dovecote of emptiness

Tea

Find yourself a cup of tea; the teapot is behind you.
Now tell me about hundreds of things

—SAKI

Should the tea be Sencha, each sip
as nuanced as grass calligraphy? Or earthy
Bancha, monkey-picked and common
as the cupboard's chipped cups?

My grandmother drank Russian Caravan
steeped in a samovar; her cup
a glass window overlooking the Saint
Petersburg winters she knew as a child.
What about a tisane of White Egret's
floating pearls?

With infinity's books opened before him
C.S. Lewis preferred to take his tea
alone; Fielding relished his with a lump of scandal.

I'm one for whom tea
conjures prayer, the kettle's whistle
a threshold into the unknown.
So let us begin with musky
Darjeeling—I've always longed
to visit Bengal, and as they say
each cup's an imaginary voyage.

Or perhaps we should give Assam a try,
its malted mystery allied with
floodplain and monsoon.
We'll drink it reverently
as Thich Nat commands,
as if each cup were the axis

on which the earth revolves.
There's time yet for those
hundreds of things.

The shadows gathering on the lawn
remind us the hours pass too quickly.
Was it last month or only yesterday
we first walked our daughters
off to school? And did I tell you
my father will be eighty on the tenth?
Yes, yes, ours is a moth's hour.
But come,
let's put the kettle on.
Even in the midst of our misting years,
that old copper pot will sing.

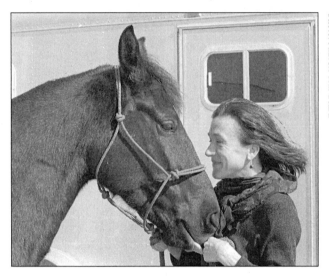

JACQUELINE KOLOSOV's previous poetry collections include *Modigliani's Muse* and *Vago*. She has also published several books of prose including two young adult novels from Hyperion/Disney. She has been awarded an NEA Literature Fellowship in Prose and a residency at the Banff Writer's Studio. Originally from Chicago, Jacqueline lives with her family, including 3 dogs—one of whom could be Toto's double—and a ½ Andalusian mare named Marah—in West Texas and is Professor of English at Texas Tech University.